Albert Speer

The Ambitious Architect of the Third

Reich – A Biography of Power, Deception,

and Reckoning

Evelyn John

"He was highly annoyed by the series of triumphs by the marvelous colored American runner, Jesse Owens. People whose antecedents came from the jungle were primitive, Hitler said with a shrug; their physiques were stronger than those of civilized whites and hence should be excluded from future games."

~ Albert Speer

Table of contents

Introduction

Albert Speer began his career as an architect but quickly became one of the most influential figures in Nazi Germany. His rise to prominence was largely due to his architectural talent, which earned him a place in Adolf Hitler's inner circle. After joining the Nazi Party in 1931, he gained recognition for his grand designs, leading to major commissions such as the Reich Chancellery and the Nazi Party rally grounds in Nuremberg. His architectural work not only demonstrated technical skill but also aligned with Hitler's vision of a powerful and imposing Reich.

In 1937, Speer was appointed General Building Inspector for Berlin, a position that granted him significant authority over urban planning. However, this role also placed him at the center of some of the regime's early oppressive policies. He was responsible for the Central Department for Resettlement, which oversaw the forced eviction of Jewish residents from their homes in Berlin. These displacements were a prelude to the mass deportations and systematic exterminations that followed as the Nazi regime escalated its persecution of Jewish communities.

Speer's ability to manage large-scale projects and optimize production processes made him an essential figure in the Nazi war effort. In February 1942, following the death of his predecessor Fritz Todt, he was appointed Reich Minister of Armaments and War Production. Under his leadership, Germany's military production increased significantly, a feat that was widely credited to his organizational skills and innovative methods. However, much of this so-called "armaments miracle" was based on misleading statistics and Nazi propaganda. The foundations of this increase in production had already been established by Todt, and Speer merely continued the work while taking credit for its success.

As Germany began facing severe setbacks on the battlefield, Speer implemented further measures to sustain arms production. In 1944, he established a task force to accelerate the manufacturing of fighter aircraft, a move that relied heavily on forced labor. Thousands of prisoners of war, concentration camp inmates, and enslaved foreign workers were subjected to inhumane conditions, forced to work in factories under brutal supervision. Speer later attempted to distance himself from these war crimes, claiming ignorance of the full extent of their suffering. However, extensive evidence links him directly to the large-scale exploitation of slave labor for the German war machine.

After Germany's defeat in 1945, Speer was arrested and put on trial at the International Military Tribunal in Nuremberg. As one of the 24 major war criminals prosecuted, he faced charges of war crimes and crimes against humanity. Unlike many other Nazi officials who remained defiant, Speer adopted a strategy of partial admission, acknowledging his role in the Nazi war effort but denying knowledge of the Holocaust. He insisted that his focus was solely on industrial matters and that he was unaware of the regime's genocidal policies. This defense, combined with his cooperative demeanor, likely spared him from execution. Instead, he was sentenced to 20 years in prison, primarily for his use of forced labor.

During his imprisonment in Spandau, Speer spent two decades writing memoirs that would later shape public perception of his role in the Nazi regime. His books, Inside the Third Reich and Spandau: The Secret Diaries, became widely read, offering a rare insider's perspective on Hitler's leadership and the inner workings of the Nazi government. Many readers viewed him as a tragic figure who had been caught up in the regime but later came to regret his involvement. By presenting himself as an apolitical technocrat who was too focused on his work to recognize the full horrors of the Holocaust, he successfully distanced himself from the worst atrocities committed by the Nazis.

For years, this carefully crafted image remained largely unchallenged, and he was often perceived as the "good Nazi" who had accepted responsibility for his actions. However, in the 1980s, historians began dismantling what became known as the "Speer myth." Researchers such as Martin Kitchen and Adam Tooze revealed that much of Speer's supposed success in boosting arms production was exaggerated. The systems that enabled increased military output had already been put in place by his predecessor, and Speer had primarily capitalized on existing structures rather than introducing groundbreaking efficiency measures.

Further evidence also emerged that contradicted his claims of ignorance regarding Nazi atrocities. Documents and testimonies indicated that he had attended high-level meetings where the "Final Solution" was discussed and had personally approved infrastructure projects linked to concentration camps. His efforts to portray himself as uninformed became increasingly implausible as historians uncovered direct links between his work and the regime's crimes. His supposed remorse and self-reflection, which had helped him gain public sympathy, were gradually exposed as a calculated attempt to rewrite his own history.

As more information came to light, the perception of Speer shifted. Once seen as an administrative genius who reluctantly served Hitler, he is now widely recognized as an ambitious figure who played a crucial role in sustaining the Nazi war effort. His extensive use of forced labor, his involvement in policies that led to the displacement and suffering of millions, and his complicity in the workings of the Nazi state reveal a far darker reality than the one he presented in his memoirs. Though he avoided execution at Nuremberg and successfully shaped public perception for decades, the historical record ultimately exposed the full extent of his involvement in the crimes of the Third Reich.

Chapter 1

Early years and personal life

Albert Speer was born in the city of Mannheim into an upper-middle-class family. His parents, Luise Mathilde Wilhelmine (Hommel) and Albert Friedrich Speer, provided him with a comfortable, if somewhat emotionally distant, upbringing. As the second of three sons, he grew up alongside his brothers, Ernst and Hermann, who frequently tormented him during his early years. This lack of warmth and affection in his household, combined with the bullying he endured from his siblings, contributed to a reserved and introspective nature that would follow him throughout his life. According to Henry T. King, a deputy prosecutor at the Nuremberg Trials who later wrote extensively about Speer, his childhood home was devoid of love and emotional support.

In 1918, as World War I was drawing to a close, Speer's family made a significant change in their living situation. They decided to lease their house in Mannheim and relocate to another property they owned in Heidelberg. This move marked a shift in young Speer's environment, though it did little to alter the distant nature of his familial relationships. Despite the emotional coldness within his household, he found solace in outdoor activities and developed a passion for sports. He became an avid skier and mountaineer, pursuits that provided him with both physical challenges and a sense of independence that was lacking in his personal life.

Following in the professional footsteps of his father and grandfather, both of whom were architects, Speer pursued a career in architecture. However, the economic turmoil of the early 1920s disrupted his educational aspirations. The hyperinflation crisis of 1923, which severely impacted Germany's economy, limited his family's financial resources, forcing him to begin his studies at the University of Karlsruhe rather than a more prestigious institution.

This decision was not due to a lack of talent or ambition but rather financial necessity. Nonetheless, his time at Karlsruhe was short-lived, as the economic situation in Germany improved in the following year.

By 1924, with the worst of the hyperinflation behind them, Speer was able to transfer to a more distinguished institution, the Technische Hochschule München, now known as the Technical University of Munich. His quest for higher education did not stop there; in 1925, he transferred again, this time to the Technische Hochschule Berlin-Charlottenburg, which is now recognized as the Technische Universität Berlin. It was at this institution that Speer found a mentor who would have a profound influence on his architectural development—Heinrich Tessenow. Tessenow, a highly regarded architect known for his minimalist and functional design philosophy, became a major source of inspiration for the young Speer.

Speer excelled under Tessenow's guidance, and after successfully passing his exams in 1927, he achieved an honor that was rare for someone so young—he was appointed as Tessenow's assistant.

This role was not merely symbolic; it allowed him to gain invaluable experience teaching classes while continuing his postgraduate studies. Working closely with Tessenow reinforced his appreciation for clean, practical architectural designs, a style that would later contrast with the grandiose and imposing structures he designed under the Nazi regime.

During his time in Munich, Speer formed a lasting friendship with Rudolf Wolters, a fellow architecture student who also studied under Tessenow. Their bond would endure for more than five decades, spanning the tumultuous years of World War II, Speer's imprisonment, and his later life. Wolters would go on to play a significant role in supporting Speer's career and legacy, particularly during and after his time as a key figure in the Nazi government.

Amidst his academic pursuits, Speer's personal life also took a significant turn. In 1922, he began a romantic relationship with Margarete (Margret) Weber, the daughter of a skilled craftsman who managed a workshop with 50 employees. Though their relationship grew serious, it was met with strong disapproval from Speer's mother, who viewed the Weber family as socially inferior.

Her class-conscious mindset made her reluctant to accept Margarete as a suitable match for her son, leading to years of tension. Despite his mother's objections, Speer remained committed to Margarete, and the couple married in Berlin on August 28, 1928.

Their marriage, however, was far from idyllic. While they would go on to have six children together, Speer's increasing involvement in professional and political affairs caused a growing emotional distance between him and his family. His dedication to his work often took precedence over his role as a husband and father, a pattern that only intensified after he joined the Nazi Party in 1931 and became deeply involved in Hitler's inner circle. By 1933, as the Nazi regime consolidated power, Speer's preoccupation with his career left little room for his family life, creating a widening rift between him and his loved ones.

Even after World War II ended and Speer was imprisoned for his role in the Nazi government, his detachment from his family remained evident. During his 20-year sentence at Spandau Prison, he focused on writing and self-reflection rather than mending his strained relationships. His memoirs, which would later become bestsellers, painted a picture of a man who had distanced himself not only from the crimes of the Nazi regime but also from the people closest to him.

After his release in 1966, his family made efforts to reconnect with him, hoping that his time in prison had given him a new perspective on the importance of personal relationships. However, despite their attempts to forge closer bonds, Speer remained emotionally reserved and somewhat aloof. His detachment, which had begun in his youth and continued throughout his career, persisted even in his later years. His professional ambitions and historical legacy seemed to occupy a larger space in his mind than his personal connections.

The trajectory of Speer's life—from an emotionally distant childhood to a career that placed ambition above personal relationships—reflected a pattern of prioritizing professional advancement over emotional engagement. His early struggles for parental approval, his mother's disapproval of his marriage, and his later disconnection from his children all point to a man who, despite his professional success, struggled to form and maintain deep personal bonds. Even as he shaped some of the most significant architectural and industrial projects of Nazi Germany, his own family remained on the periphery of his life, unable to break through the emotional walls he had built.

Albert Speer's story is not just one of political and historical significance but also one of personal estrangement. While he played a crucial role in Nazi Germany's architectural and industrial efforts, his legacy is also marked by his inability—or unwillingness—to foster meaningful relationships with those closest to him. Whether due to the emotional coldness of his upbringing or his own personal choices, he remained a figure who, even in his later years, was more connected to his past than to his present.

Chapter 2

Party architect and government functionary

In January 1931, Albert Speer took the first step toward what would become a defining chapter in his life by applying for membership in the Nazi Party. On March 1 of that year, he was officially registered as member number 474,481. At the time, Germany was in the grip of the Great Depression, and economic instability had made professional opportunities scarce. Speer, who had been working as an assistant to his former professor Heinrich Tessenow, found that his stipend was shrinking due to financial constraints. Faced with an uncertain future, he made the difficult decision to leave his position and return to his hometown of

Mannheim, hoping to establish himself as an independent architect. However, despite his education and training, he struggled to secure commissions. With his architectural career failing to gain traction, his father intervened, offering him a part-time position managing the family's real estate holdings.

Speer's association with the Nazi Party initially seemed more practical than ideological. In July 1932, during the buildup to the Reichstag elections, he and his family traveled to Berlin to assist the Party in its campaign efforts. It was during this period that he made an important connection—Karl Hanke, a Nazi official and an acquaintance of Speer, recognized his potential and recommended him for a small but significant project. Joseph Goebbels, the Nazi propaganda chief, needed an architect to renovate the Party's headquarters in Berlin. Hanke suggested Speer for the job, and the young architect accepted the commission. After completing the renovation, Speer returned to Mannheim and remained there even as Adolf Hitler rose to power in January 1933.

The turning point in Speer's career came later that year when he was invited to submit designs for the 1933 Nuremberg Rally.

These rallies were massive propaganda spectacles meant to showcase Nazi strength and unity, and Speer's work on the project brought him into direct contact with Hitler for the first time. The rally organizers, uncertain about whether to approve Speer's designs, deferred the decision to Rudolf Hess, who in turn sent Speer to Hitler's Munich apartment to seek his approval personally. This initial meeting proved to be a pivotal moment in Speer's life. Hitler was impressed with his architectural vision, and shortly afterward, Speer was appointed as the Nazi Party's Commissioner for the Artistic and Technical Presentation of Party Rallies and Demonstrations.

Speer's association with Hitler quickly deepened. As the newly appointed Chancellor, Hitler was eager to transform the Reich Chancellery into a symbol of his power. At the end of 1933, he selected the experienced architect Paul Troost to lead the renovation of the building. However, having been impressed with Speer's earlier work for Goebbels, Hitler assigned him the crucial task of managing the construction site under Troost's supervision. This project brought Speer into close proximity with Hitler, who resided in the Chancellery and visited the site daily. Speer and the construction supervisors regularly briefed him on progress, and after one such meeting, Hitler extended a personal invitation for lunch—an invitation that Speer eagerly accepted.

This moment marked the beginning of Speer's rapid ascent within the Nazi hierarchy. Hitler took a personal liking to him, drawn not only to his architectural talent but also to his reserved and efficient demeanor. Over time, Speer became part of Hitler's inner circle. He was frequently summoned for morning walks or private discussions, during which Hitler would share his grand visions for Germany's architectural future. Unlike many of Hitler's other associates, who were primarily military officers or political operatives, Speer's presence in these conversations was driven by his technical expertise rather than ideological fervor. However, the trust and access he gained would soon translate into significant political power.

Speer's memoirs, written years later after the war, portray him as a reluctant participant in Nazi politics. In the English version of his writings, he minimized his involvement, claiming that his commitment to the Party was limited to merely paying his monthly dues. He attempted to present himself as an apolitical professional who had been drawn in by circumstances rather than conviction. However, in the German version of his memoirs, he was more forthcoming, acknowledging that he saw the Nazi Party as offering a "new mission" for Germany. In an interview with William Hamsher, he provided an even clearer rationale, stating that he had joined the Party as a means of protecting Germany from Communism, a sentiment that resonated with many middle-class professionals at the time.

Despite these claims, historians have challenged the idea that Speer was a passive or reluctant Nazi. While he did not deliver fiery anti-Semitic speeches like many of his contemporaries, his actions demonstrated his complicity in the regime's racist policies. Historian Magnus Brechtken has pointed out that Speer's involvement in Nazi projects, particularly those that displaced Jewish residents and exploited forced labor, speaks louder than his later justifications. Brechtken argued that Speer's motivations were primarily driven by a desire for power, influence, and financial gain rather than ideological commitment. Nevertheless, the end result was the same—his architectural and administrative contributions directly furthered the goals of the Nazi regime.

One of the most revealing aspects of Speer's rise was his ability to navigate the dangerous political landscape of Nazi Germany without appearing overly ambitious. Unlike other high-ranking Nazis who schemed and plotted against one another for Hitler's favor, Speer maintained an image of a diligent and apolitical expert. This allowed him to gain Hitler's trust while avoiding the internal power struggles that plagued the regime. As a result, he secured numerous high-profile commissions and continued to expand his influence, eventually rising to the position of Reich Minister of Armaments and War Production.

Looking back at Speer's early years in the Nazi Party, it becomes clear that his ascent was not a matter of mere chance or circumstance. While he may have initially joined the Party without deep ideological conviction, he quickly recognized the opportunities it presented. His architectural talent and ability to impress Hitler gave him access to unprecedented power, and he capitalized on it without hesitation. Though he later attempted to distance himself from the crimes of the Third Reich, his direct involvement in projects that contributed to Nazi oppression cannot be ignored.

Speer's story serves as an example of how technical expertise and ambition, when placed in the service of an authoritarian regime, can lead to moral compromise. Whether or not he fully believed in Nazi ideology, his willingness to align himself with the Party for personal and professional gain ensured that his legacy would forever be tied to one of history's darkest periods.

Following the death of Paul Troost on January 21, 1934, Albert Speer quickly stepped into his mentor's role, becoming the de facto chief architect of the Nazi Party. Recognizing his talent and unwavering dedication, Hitler appointed him as the head of the Chief Office for Construction. While this position officially placed him under the authority of Rudolf Hess, in practice, it granted Speer significant autonomy and influence over the architectural projects that would define the visual identity of Nazi Germany.

One of Speer's first major projects after assuming this role was the design of the Zeppelinfeld stadium in Nuremberg. This colossal structure was specifically intended to serve as the centerpiece for the Party's annual rallies, which were grandiose propaganda spectacles aimed at displaying Nazi power and unity. The stadium, capable of accommodating an astounding 340,000 spectators, became an iconic backdrop for these events and was prominently featured in Leni Riefenstahl's propaganda film Triumph of the Will. To enhance the dramatic impact of these gatherings, Speer advocated for as many nighttime events as possible. This allowed him to incorporate his famous "Cathedral of Light" effect, a striking visual display where hundreds of anti-aircraft searchlights projected beams of light into the sky, creating an ethereal, cathedral-like atmosphere. While this was largely a theatrical choice to heighten the rallies' grandeur, some accounts suggest that Speer also preferred night events as a way to obscure the presence of overweight Nazi officials from public view.

Beyond the Zeppelinfeld, Nuremberg was envisioned as the architectural heart of the Nazi movement, with plans for numerous monumental structures that were never realized.

Among these was the proposed German Stadium, which, had it been completed, would have been the largest stadium in the world, accommodating a staggering 400,000 spectators. Speer's projects reflected Hitler's obsession with scale and permanence, as he favored imposing structures made from stone, which he believed would stand the test of time and serve as a lasting testament to the Third Reich's supposed greatness.

In addition to his work in Nuremberg, Speer was tasked with refining Werner March's design for the Olympic Stadium in Berlin, which was under construction for the 1936 Summer Olympics. His modifications, including the addition of a stone façade, aligned with Hitler's aesthetic preferences and helped to solidify Speer's reputation as the regime's foremost architect. His growing prominence led to another prestigious assignment—the design of the German Pavilion for the 1937 International Exposition in Paris. This structure, intended to showcase Nazi Germany's cultural and technological achievements, stood in direct competition with the Soviet Pavilion, symbolizing the ideological rivalry between the two nations on an architectural stage.

On January 30, 1937, Adolf Hitler elevated Albert Speer to the influential position of General Building Inspector for the Reich Capital. This appointment came with the rank of State Secretary in the Reich government, giving Speer significant power over Berlin's urban planning and development. Unlike the city's mayor or its Gauleiter, who were accountable to the Party's hierarchy, Speer reported directly to Hitler, reinforcing his growing status within the Nazi leadership. With this newfound authority, Hitler entrusted him with the ambitious task of redesigning Berlin into a grand imperial capital that would symbolize the strength and permanence of the Third Reich.

At the heart of Speer's plans for Berlin was the transformation of the city's landscape through a three-mile-long grand boulevard, which he referred to as the Prachtstraße, or the "Street of Magnificence." Later known as the "North–South Axis," this massive thoroughfare was designed to be a showpiece of Nazi architecture. At its northern end, Speer envisioned the Volkshalle, a massive domed assembly hall that would tower over the city at over 700 feet (210 meters) in height, with enough floor space to accommodate an astounding 180,000 people. Hitler, inspired by the ancient Pantheon in Rome, saw the Volkshalle as a structure that would embody the power and eternity of Nazi rule. At the southern end of the axis, Speer planned an equally imposing triumphal arch, nearly 400 feet (120 meters) high—large enough to encompass the Arc de Triomphe in Paris within its opening. To further streamline Berlin's transformation, existing railway stations were to be demolished and replaced with two enormous new terminals.

Speer's vision required an extensive overhaul of Berlin's urban layout, and to execute this massive project, he enlisted his longtime associate Rudolf Wolters, who was given primary responsibility for designing the Prachtstraße. Despite its ambitious scope, the outbreak of World War II in 1939 put the Berlin redevelopment plan on hold. With Germany's resources increasingly diverted to military production and the war effort, the grand vision for the Reich's capital was never fully realized. Reflecting on these projects years later, Speer himself acknowledged that many of his architectural ideas, which once enthralled Nazi leadership, were impractical and, in his own words, "awful."

While the Berlin project stalled, another of Speer's major undertakings—the construction of a new Reich Chancellery—moved forward. Hitler had been dissatisfied with the existing Reich Chancellery as early as 1934 and had initiated plans for a complete reconstruction. By March 1936, the first buildings were demolished to make way for a grand new complex on Voßstraße. Speer, involved from the beginning, had already been assigned the renovation of the Borsig Palace on Wilhelmstraße, which was to serve as the headquarters for the Sturmabteilung (SA) following the purge of the Night of the Long Knives.

By May 1936, Speer had completed the preliminary work on the new Reich Chancellery. In June of that year, he charged a personal honorarium of 30,000 Reichsmarks for his services and projected that the project would take three to four years to complete. By July 1937, the detailed plans were finalized, and construction commenced with intense urgency. The first shell of the building was completed on January 1, 1938. Less than a month later, on January 27, Hitler granted Speer plenipotentiary powers, giving him unrestricted authority to ensure the Chancellery's completion by January 1, 1939.

Despite the enormous scale of the project, Hitler wanted to portray the Reich's efficiency and power, so he claimed during a ceremonial event on August 2, 1938, that Speer had been ordered to complete the building within the year. This unrealistic demand led to grueling labor conditions, with workers forced to toil in ten-to-twelve-hour shifts. Due to labor shortages, the SS established two new concentration camps in 1938, where prisoners were forced to quarry stone for the Chancellery's construction. Additionally, a brick factory was built near the Oranienburg concentration camp under Speer's direction. When concerns were raised about the appalling conditions at the factory, Speer dismissed them with a chilling remark: "The Yids got used to making bricks while in Egyptian captivity."

By early January 1939, the Reich Chancellery was complete. Hitler viewed the building as one of his greatest achievements, calling it the "crowning glory of the greater German political empire." The new Chancellery was meant to symbolize Nazi strength and permanence, with long marble corridors and a grand reception hall designed to intimidate foreign diplomats and visitors.

During this period, one of the most infamous events of the Nazi regime took place—the Kristallnacht pogrom on November 9–10, 1938. While Jewish-owned businesses, synagogues, and homes were ransacked and burned throughout Germany, Speer remained silent. In his memoir, Inside the Third Reich, he initially omitted any mention of Kristallnacht. It was only at the insistence of his publisher that he briefly added a reference to seeing the charred remains of the Central Synagogue in Berlin from his car window.

Beyond ignoring the violence against Jews, Speer played an active role in their persecution. His position as General Building Inspector gave him significant control over housing in Berlin, and from 1939 onward, he used this authority to evict Jewish tenants from their homes. Under the pretext of implementing Nazi racial laws, his office displaced at least 75,000 Jewish residents, ostensibly to make room for non-Jewish tenants who had been displaced by urban redevelopment or wartime bombings. While Speer later claimed he had no knowledge of what happened to the evicted

Jews, he admitted seeing crowds of Jewish families at the Nikolassee railroad station, waiting for transport to an unknown destination. He later wrote, "I am sure that an oppressive feeling struck me as I drove past. I presumably had a sense of somber events." Historian Matthias Schmidt, however, found Speer's denials absurd, noting that he had personally visited concentration camps and was well aware of their purpose. Likewise, historian Martin Kitchen dismissed Speer's claims of ignorance, stating that he was not just a passive observer but an active participant in the Nazi regime's crimes.

With the outbreak of World War II in September 1939, Speer's role in Berlin's urban planning took a backseat to the war effort. He organized quick-reaction squads tasked with clearing rubble and constructing roads to aid the military. Over time, these units were repurposed to manage bomb-damaged sites after Allied air raids. However, Speer's use of forced labor did not diminish—instead, it expanded. Jewish laborers, along with foreign workers and concentration camp prisoners, were forced to work under inhumane conditions on Speer's various construction projects.

While his grand architectural plans for Berlin and Nuremberg were put on hold due to wartime constraints, Speer continued to oversee construction projects for the military and the SS. His office played a crucial role in building infrastructure for the German war machine, including air raid shelters, fortifications, and weapons production facilities. By leveraging forced labor, Speer amassed significant wealth, becoming one of the richest members of the Nazi elite.

Despite his later attempts to portray himself as an apolitical technocrat who had been swept up in the tide of history, Speer's actions during this period paint a different picture. He was not just an ambitious architect; he was an active enabler of the Nazi regime's crimes, profiting from forced labor and playing a direct role in the persecution of Jews. His willingness to align himself with Hitler's vision, no matter the human cost, cemented his place as one of the key figures in the Third Reich's leadership.

Chapter 3

Minister of Armaments

Albert Speer, one of the youngest and most ambitious figures in Adolf Hitler's inner circle, steadily ascended the ranks of the Nazi hierarchy, gaining unprecedented power within the regime. By 1938, his influence had expanded significantly when Hermann Göring, then the Prussian Minister President, appointed him to the Prussian State Council. Speer's political career further advanced in 1941 when he was elected to the Reichstag, representing electoral constituency 2 (Berlin–West). His rise, however, took a dramatic turn in 1942, following the unexpected death of Reich Minister of Armaments and Munitions, Fritz Todt.

On February 8, 1942, Todt perished in a plane crash shortly after departing from Hitler's eastern headquarters in Rastenburg. The night before, Speer had been invited to accompany Todt on the flight to Berlin but declined at the last minute due to an extended late-night meeting with Hitler. The accident presented an immediate power vacuum, and Hitler wasted no time in appointing Speer as Todt's successor. British historian Martin Kitchen later noted that this appointment was unsurprising, given Speer's unwavering loyalty to Hitler and his extensive experience in overseeing construction projects, including prisoner-of-war camps and military infrastructure.

Speer did not just inherit Todt's ministerial role; he also assumed control of a host of influential positions, including Inspector General of German Roadways, Inspector General for Water and Energy, and Head of the Nazi Party's Office of Technology. Additionally, he was placed in charge of Organisation Todt, a massive state-run construction company responsible for key military and industrial projects. Despite these prestigious titles, Hitler did not provide Speer with a clearly defined scope of authority. Instead, Speer was left to navigate the ruthless Nazi bureaucracy, where he had to contend with political rivals to consolidate his influence.

One of Speer's immediate goals was to extend his control beyond armaments for the army to include production for all branches of the military. His push for centralized authority faced resistance from Göring, who oversaw the Four Year Plan, but Speer ultimately secured Hitler's backing. On March 1, 1942, Göring signed a decree officially naming Speer "General Plenipotentiary for Armament Tasks" within the Four Year Plan. This was a significant victory, as it allowed Speer to streamline Germany's war production and consolidate resources under his leadership.

Speer's next strategic move came in April 1942 when he persuaded Göring to establish a three-member Central Planning Board within the Four Year Plan. This board granted him supreme authority over the procurement and allocation of raw materials, as well as production scheduling. With these measures, Speer successfully centralized German war production under a single agency, securing an unprecedented level of control over the Reich's military-industrial complex.

At the time, and even in the post-war years, Speer was widely credited with orchestrating an "armaments miracle." Under his leadership, German war production significantly increased, despite the ongoing challenges of World War II. However, historians have since questioned the extent of his contributions. Some argue that the groundwork for increased production had already been laid under Todt. Furthermore, naval armaments did not come under Speer's jurisdiction until October 1943, and Luftwaffe production remained independent until June 1944—yet both sectors experienced similar growth rates despite initially being outside his control. Additionally, increased coal allocations to the steel industry played a major role in boosting ammunition production.

While production peaked between June and July 1944, Speer faced a critical challenge: fuel shortages. By August 1944, Germany had lost access to Romanian oil fields, leading to a dramatic decline in fuel availability. Despite the increased production of tanks, aircraft, and artillery, the lack of fuel rendered much of Germany's war machinery useless. Without sufficient resources, offensive military operations became nearly impossible, and vast stockpiles of weapons sat idle.

As Minister of Armaments, Speer was responsible for ensuring that the German army received the weapons it needed. He prioritized tank production with Hitler's full support, yet his efforts were hindered by the Führer's constant interference. Hitler frequently changed his mind regarding tank specifications, causing delays and inefficiencies. As a result, despite the supposed high priority of tank production, a relatively small percentage of the armaments budget was allocated to it. This mismanagement contributed to significant German failures, most notably during the Battle of Prokhorovka, a crucial confrontation on the Eastern Front that marked a turning point in the war against the Soviet Red Army.

Beyond his role in armaments production, Speer played a direct role in the Nazi regime's atrocities. As head of Organisation Todt, he was deeply involved in the construction and expansion of concentration camps. He personally approved an allocation of 13.7 million Reichsmarks to expand Auschwitz and other camps, enabling the construction of 300 additional barracks. This expansion increased Auschwitz's capacity to 132,000 prisoners. The funds also covered the construction of gas chambers, crematoria, and morgues—facilities specifically designed for mass murder. The SS referred to this initiative as "Professor Speer's Special Programme."

As the war escalated, labor shortages became a major problem for Speer's war economy. By 1943, Germany had conscripted over six million workers into the armed forces, leaving a severe deficit in industrial labor. To address this issue, Hitler appointed Fritz Sauckel as a "manpower dictator" responsible for securing additional workers. Sauckel and Speer worked closely together, and Speer enthusiastically supported Sauckel's brutal recruitment methods.

Speer formally requested one million "voluntary" laborers to meet the demands of the armaments industry. However, Sauckel resorted to mass forced labor programs, rounding up civilians from occupied countries such as France, Holland, and Belgium. Entire villages were emptied, with men and women forcibly transported to Germany to work in armaments factories under deplorable conditions. In Soviet-occupied territories, the situation was even more severe—any civilian areas suspected of harboring partisans were subjected to mass roundups, with inhabitants forcibly shipped to Germany as laborers.

By April 1943, Sauckel had provided Speer's industrial sector with 1,568,801 forced laborers, including prisoners of war and concentration camp detainees. These workers were subjected to extreme exploitation, enduring grueling hours, starvation, and exposure to brutal conditions. Many perished due to exhaustion, disease, or outright execution. It was Speer's direct involvement in the Nazi forced labor system that led to his conviction at the Nuremberg Trials.

Despite his later claims of ignorance regarding the atrocities of the Nazi regime, Speer's deep entanglement in the exploitation of forced labor and the expansion of extermination camps proves otherwise. He was not merely an apolitical technocrat but an active enabler of Nazi crimes. His ambition, combined with his willingness to comply with Hitler's most inhumane policies, solidified his role as a central figure in the machinery of the Third Reich.

Albert Speer's rise to power as Minister of Armaments marked a pivotal moment in Nazi Germany's war economy, cementing his influence within Adolf Hitler's inner circle. Initially, Speer was responsible for overseeing the production of armaments for the German Army. However, his ambitions far exceeded these responsibilities, and he soon sought control over the armaments production for the Luftwaffe (Air Force) and Kriegsmarine (Navy) as well. Speer's approach was characterized by an unexpected and intense drive for power, and his close relationship with Hitler offered him political protection that allowed him to outwit and outmaneuver rivals within the regime. Despite disapproval from Hitler's cabinet members, Speer succeeded in expanding his reach and consolidating more control over the war economy.

By July 1943, Speer had achieved control over armaments production for the Luftwaffe and Kriegsmarine. His influence continued to grow as he took command of most of the Ministry of Economics, ultimately earning the title of "Reich Minister for

Armaments and War Production" on September 2, 1943. This promotion marked him as one of the most powerful individuals in Nazi Germany. With this new role, Speer could shape the direction of the war effort and dictate the industrial and military production strategies that would determine Germany's ability to sustain itself in the ongoing conflict.

Speer's ambitions were not limited to high-level control; he sought to bring about a revolution in the methods and practices used in the production of armaments. He believed that the shipbuilding industry was being hindered by outdated techniques and that innovative approaches could vastly improve output. Speer and his chosen director of submarine construction, Otto Merker, pushed for a more modernized approach, focusing on the prefabrication of sections for the Kriegsmarine's new generation of submarines, the Type XXI and Type XXIII. Instead of constructing submarines in traditional shipyards, Speer envisioned these submarines being built at various facilities and then assembled into complete units. However, this method ultimately proved to be flawed. The design and construction processes were rushed, leading to critical production delays and errors that crippled the submarines. While dozens of these submarines were constructed, very few were ever operational, significantly undermining the importance of the program.

Despite these setbacks, Speer's ability to maintain his position and expand his influence was remarkable. However, in December 1943, his leadership was temporarily interrupted when an accident in Lapland caused him to severely damage his knee, which incapacitated him for several months. During this time, Speer was under the care of Professor Karl Gebhardt, a controversial figure with connections to Nazi atrocities, further complicating Speer's political standing. In mid-January 1944, Speer's health deteriorated further when he suffered a lung embolism. He remained bedridden for a time but was determined to retain his power. Rather than appoint a deputy, Speer continued to direct operations from his sickbed, an indication of his desire to maintain full control of the Ministry of Armaments.

Speer's illness coincided with a significant blow to the German war effort. The Allied "Big Week" bombing raids, launched in early 1944, targeted German aircraft factories, severely disrupting the production of fighter planes. This event provided an opportunity for Speer's political rivals to undermine his authority and diminish his standing with Hitler. His inability to manage the consequences of the Allied attacks caused Speer to lose much of his influence, and his relationship with Hitler, once unshakable, began to weaken.

In response to the damage inflicted on the German aviation industry, Hitler authorized the creation of the Fighter Staff, a task force designed to preserve and expand the production of fighter aircraft. Speer, who had once been the uncontested authority on armaments production, saw his control eroded as the Fighter Staff was established by March 1, 1944. Speer's rival Erhard Milch, who served in the Reich Aviation Ministry, played a key role in supporting the Fighter Staff's formation. By mid-1944, German fighter aircraft production had more than doubled, although much of this increase came from outdated models that were easy targets for Allied forces. Despite Speer's original vision for the war economy, the increased production was not enough to overcome the strategic disadvantages faced by Germany.

The Fighter Staff initiative also marked an expansion of forced labor within the German war economy. The SS provided tens of thousands of prisoners from concentration camps to work on various projects for companies such as Junkers, Messerschmitt, and BMW. In order to maximize production, Speer implemented a brutal system of punishments for workers, including those who feigned illness, slowed down production, or attempted to escape. These workers were subjected to extreme physical punishment, and many were sent to concentration camps. In 1944, the system of forced labor reached its peak, with over half a million workers arrested and coerced into labor. Speer's underground factories, designed to keep production going despite Allied bombing campaigns, were death traps. Over 140,000 workers were employed in these factories, where conditions were so harsh that regular executions were carried out to maintain discipline. The Dora underground factory, for example, had so many corpses that its crematorium could not keep up with the demand.

Under Speer's guidance, the most significant technological advancement was the development of Germany's rocket program. Initially started in 1932, the rocket program had not yet produced any significant weaponry. Speer saw its potential and eagerly supported the project. In March 1942, he ordered the production of A4 rockets, the precursor to the world's first ballistic missile, the V-2 rocket. These rockets were developed at Peenemünde and were intended to strike major Allied cities, with the first V-2 missile aimed at Paris on September 8, 1944. While the rocket program was technologically advanced, it proved to be a drain on the war economy. The significant capital invested in the development and production of these rockets was not offset by their effectiveness in combat. Moreover, the rockets were assembled at the Mittelwerk underground factory, using forced labor from the Mittelbau-Dora concentration camp. Of the 60,000 prisoners sent to the camp, 20,000 perished due to the appalling working conditions.

By 1944, Speer's authority continued to wane. On April 14, he lost control of Organisation Todt to his deputy, Franz Xaver Dorsch. Later, Speer was not involved in the 20 July assassination attempt against Hitler but played a minor role in the aftermath when Hitler survived. This incident, along with subsequent political maneuvering, led to further losses of power for Speer as his rivals successfully attacked some of his closest allies. As radical elements within the Nazi Party grew in influence, Speer's management system fell out of favor, and his grip on power loosened considerably.

By late 1944, Nazi Germany was rapidly crumbling under the weight of territorial losses and the intensified Allied bombing campaign. The German economy, already strained by years of war, began to collapse as Allied air raids systematically targeted key infrastructure. The destruction of the transportation network proved especially devastating, severing essential supply lines that connected industrial centers with coal and raw materials necessary for armaments production. Without these vital resources, German war production began to grind to a halt.

Despite these mounting setbacks, Albert Speer, as Minister of Armaments and War Production, remained optimistic, at least outwardly. In January 1945, he reassured Joseph Goebbels that Germany could sustain armaments production for another year. However, his confidence was short-lived. Later that same month, the Soviet capture of the Silesian industrial region—a key hub of German industry—forced him to recognize the inevitable:

Germany was on the brink of total defeat. Despite this realization, Speer did not immediately advocate for surrender. Instead, he argued that prolonging the war could still be strategically beneficial, hoping that by holding out longer, Germany might negotiate better terms with the Allies instead of facing unconditional surrender.

During the early months of 1945, Speer attempted to maintain an illusion of control. He assured Hitler and other high-ranking officials that his ministry would soon provide "decisive weapons" and increase armaments production significantly, supposedly shifting the balance of power on the battlefield. In February, he gained control over the German railway system and enlisted Heinrich Himmler to supply concentration camp prisoners to assist in repairing the damaged network. However, by mid-March, it had become clear to him that Germany's economy was in freefall and would likely collapse completely within two months.

Speer began working to mitigate the destruction that would accompany Germany's downfall. While he still publicly supported the war effort, he sought to prevent the total devastation of

German industry and infrastructure. On March 15, he presented Hitler with a memorandum detailing the dire state of the economy and requested permission to halt the destruction of facilities that could be useful after the war. Just days later, he proposed that Germany concentrate its remaining military forces along the Rhine and Vistula rivers to prolong the conflict, though such a strategy ignored the reality that the German military was vastly outmatched and could not withstand the Allies' overwhelming firepower.

Hitler, however, had no interest in Speer's proposals to preserve infrastructure. On March 19, he issued the infamous "Nero Decree," ordering the systematic destruction of Germany's remaining industrial and transportation facilities to deny them to the advancing Allies. Horrified by this directive, Speer worked behind the scenes to persuade military leaders and Nazi officials to disregard the order. His efforts were largely successful, and by March 28–29, he met with Hitler and convinced him to rescind the decree, granting Speer authority over demolitions. However, some German forces continued to destroy bridges and infrastructure despite this reversal.

By April, Germany's armaments industry had effectively ceased to exist, and Speer had little to do in his official capacity. On April 22, he visited the Führerbunker in Berlin for the final time. He met briefly with Hitler, toured the heavily damaged Reich Chancellery, and then left for Hamburg. In later years, Speer would claim in his memoirs that he confessed to Hitler that he had been actively disobeying the scorched-earth policy, a statement that historians like Richard J. Evans have dismissed as fictionalized self-aggrandizement.

As the war neared its conclusion, Hitler dictated his final political testament on April 29, just one day before taking his own life. In this document, he removed Speer from any future government role, instead naming his subordinate, Karl-Otto Saur, as his replacement. This decision deeply disappointed Speer, who had harbored hopes of playing a key role in post-war Germany.

After Hitler's death, Karl Dönitz, who had been appointed as Hitler's successor, sought to form a functioning government in the war's final days. Speer offered his services and was appointed Minister of Industry and Production in the newly formed

Flensburg Government on May 5. This short-lived administration, led by Lutz Graf Schwerin von Krosigk, attempted to manage Germany's surrender and transition in the immediate aftermath of Hitler's regime. Beginning on May 10, Speer began cooperating with the Allies, providing intelligence on the effects of the air war and other matters of interest. However, this cooperation did not spare him from arrest. On May 23, British forces detained Speer along with other members of the Flensburg Government, formally bringing Nazi Germany to an end.

Chapter 4

Post-war

After his arrest, Albert Speer was moved through several internment centers where he was rigorously interrogated about his role in the Nazi regime. By September 1945, he was officially informed that he would be put on trial for war crimes. Shortly thereafter, he was transported to Nuremberg, where he was incarcerated alongside other high-ranking Nazi officials awaiting prosecution. The charges against him were severe, encompassing four major counts: conspiracy to commit crimes against peace, planning and waging wars of aggression, war crimes, and crimes against humanity. These charges reflected his significant role in the

Nazi war effort, particularly in the armaments industry, which had relied heavily on forced labor.

At the trial, the chief U.S. prosecutor, Robert H. Jackson, condemned Speer's actions, stating that he had actively participated in the systematic exploitation of prisoners of war and foreign workers. Jackson argued that while Speer's ministry thrived, producing vast amounts of weapons and military equipment, the enslaved workers toiling under brutal conditions suffered from starvation and abuse. Despite these damning accusations, Speer's defense strategy was notably different from that of many of his co-defendants. His attorney, Hans Flächsner, carefully crafted an image of Speer as a technocrat—an apolitical architect-turned-minister who had been swept into the Nazi hierarchy without harboring ideological convictions. Unlike other defendants who remained defiant or sought to justify their actions, Speer positioned himself as a remorseful figure, acknowledging his moral responsibility while denying knowledge of the regime's most heinous crimes. This strategic approach helped to distinguish him from individuals like Hermann Göring and Heinrich Himmler, who were deeply entrenched in Nazi ideology.

When the verdict was delivered on October 1, 1946, Speer was found guilty of war crimes and crimes against humanity, primarily due to his exploitation of forced labor. However, he was acquitted of the charges related to initiating aggressive war and conspiracy to commit crimes against peace. His repeated claims that he had been unaware of the Nazi extermination policies contributed to this outcome, as the prosecution lacked definitive evidence to prove otherwise. Decades later, a private letter from Speer written in 1971—revealed publicly in 2007—contradicted his claims, suggesting that he had indeed known about the mass killings.

The sentencing of Speer was a subject of intense debate among the tribunal judges. While three out of the eight judges, including two Soviet representatives and American judge Francis Biddle, pushed for the death penalty, the rest were divided. After two days of deliberation, a compromise was reached, and Speer was sentenced to 20 years in prison, a punishment that allowed him to escape execution but ensured his prolonged confinement.

On July 18, 1947, Albert Speer was transferred to Spandau Prison in Berlin to begin serving his 20-year sentence. Within the prison, he was simply known as Prisoner Number Five, stripped of his former titles and power. While incarcerated, Speer faced significant personal losses, including the deaths of both his parents. His father, who had always despised the Nazi regime and had shown silent contempt when introduced to Hitler, passed away in 1947, shortly after Speer's imprisonment. His mother, in contrast, had been a devoted Nazi supporter who enjoyed socializing with Hitler, and she passed away in 1952. Despite his confinement, Speer maintained connections with the outside world through his closest allies. His longtime secretary, Annemarie Kempf, and his friend, Rudolf Wolters, were prohibited from direct correspondence but found ways to assist his family. Speer was officially allowed to send letters only to his wife, but he managed to smuggle additional messages and writings out of prison with the help of a sympathetic Dutch orderly, Toni Proost, who began aiding him in 1948.

In 1949, Wolters took further steps to support Speer by opening a bank account in his name and raising funds from architects and industrialists who had once benefited from Speer's wartime activities. Initially, the money was used to provide financial support for Speer's family, ensuring they could maintain a decent standard of living. However, as time went on, the funds served additional purposes, including paying for Provost's vacations and bribing individuals who might influence Speer's early release. Once Speer became aware of the fund, he took a direct role in managing it, issuing detailed instructions on its use. Over the final 17 years of his imprisonment, Wolters successfully raised 158,000 Deutsche Marks for him.

Prison regulations forbade inmates from writing memoirs, but Speer was determined to document his experiences. Through secret channels, he managed to smuggle thousands of pages of his writings to Wolters. By November 1953, he had completed his memoirs, which later served as the foundation for Inside the Third Reich, his well-known autobiographical work. In Spandau Diaries, Speer sought to portray himself as a tragic figure—a man who had struck a Faustian bargain and was now paying the price with years of incarceration.

To endure the long years in prison, Speer focused on maintaining both his physical and mental health. Spandau Prison had a large yard where each inmate was assigned a plot of land for gardening. Speer took great care in cultivating his section, transforming it into a lush garden with flower beds, shrubs, fruit trees, and well-manicured lawns. In addition to gardening, he devised a unique way to keep his daily walks interesting—an imaginary journey around the world. Beginning in Berlin, he mentally charted a path across Eurasia, crossed the Bering Strait into Alaska, and traveled down the western coast of North America, carefully measuring distances to match real-world geography. By the time his sentence ended, he had theoretically reached Guadalajara, Mexico, having "walked" over 30,000 kilometers. He also spent much of his time reading, studying architectural journals, and refining his knowledge of English and French. Speer later claimed to have read 5,000 books during his imprisonment, though given the length of his sentence—7,305 days—this would mean finishing a book every one and a half days.

Throughout his imprisonment, various influential figures called for his early release. Notably, French President Charles de Gaulle and American diplomat George Wildman Ball supported the idea of commuting his sentence. In Germany, Willy Brandt also advocated for his release and helped halt de-Nazification proceedings against him, which could have resulted in the confiscation of his property. However, these efforts were ultimately unsuccessful. The Soviet Union, having initially pushed for Speer's execution at the Nuremberg Trials, remained firmly opposed to any reduction of his sentence. As a result, Speer served the entirety of his 20-year term and was finally released from Spandau Prison at midnight on October 1, 1966.

Albert Speer's release from Spandau Prison on October 1, 1966, was a highly publicized event that attracted global media attention. Reporters, photographers, and curious onlookers gathered outside the prison and later at the Hotel Berlin, where Speer spent his first night of freedom. Despite the media frenzy, he chose to remain relatively silent, only making extensive remarks in a major interview with Der Spiegel in November of that year. Initially, Speer expressed a desire to resume his career as an architect, but his only project—a partnership to design a brewery—failed to materialize. Instead, he turned to writing, revising his Spandau notes into two widely read autobiographies: Inside the Third Reich (Erinnerungen in German) and Spandau: The Secret Diaries. He later published a study on Heinrich Himmler and the SS, which appeared in English under titles such as The Slave State: Heinrich Himmler's Masterplan for SS Supremacy and Infiltration: How Heinrich Himmler Schemed to Build an SS Industrial Empire. These works were shaped with the assistance of historians and publishers, including Joachim Fest and Wolf Jobst Siedler.

Despite his public reinvention, Speer struggled to reconnect with his family. His son, Albert Jr., who had followed in his father's architectural footsteps, remained distant, and his daughter Hilde Schramm later recounted that one by one, her siblings gave up on trying to rebuild a relationship with their father. Speer did provide financial assistance to his brother Hermann after the war, but his other brother, Ernst, died in the Battle of Stalingrad—despite repeated pleas from their parents for Speer to use his influence to bring him home.

In an effort to preserve his legacy, Speer donated Chronicle, his personal diary, to the German Federal Archives. However, this version had been carefully edited by his close associate Rudolf Wolters to omit any mention of the Holocaust or the Nazi regime's atrocities. Historian David Irving later uncovered inconsistencies between this sanitized version and independent documents. When Speer learned of these discrepancies, he urged Wolters to destroy the unedited material, but Wolters refused. Their relationship soured, and a year before Speer's death, Wolters granted historian Matthias Schmidt access to the original records. Schmidt subsequently published the first book that critically dismantled Speer's carefully crafted narrative.

Speer's memoirs became instant bestsellers, captivating the public with an insider's perspective on Nazi Germany. His ability to frame himself as an apolitical technocrat who had merely "followed orders" resonated with many former Nazis and ordinary Germans, offering them an alibi for their own involvement in the regime. This "Speer myth" gained significant traction, further reinforced by his publishers and supporters, even as new historical evidence emerged that contradicted his claims.

Throughout his later years, Albert Speer remained highly accessible to historians, journalists, and researchers, eager to present his version of history. He frequently granted interviews and engaged in discussions about his role in the Nazi regime, carefully shaping his public image. In October 1973, he made his first visit to the United Kingdom, traveling to London for an appearance on the BBC's Midweek program, where he spoke about his experiences. That same year, he was also featured in The World at War, a groundbreaking television documentary series that explored the history of World War II. His willingness to discuss his past allowed him to maintain a degree of public interest, and he continued to engage with the media in the following years.

In 1981, Speer returned to London to participate in an interview for the BBC's Newsnight program. However, during his stay, he suffered a stroke and passed away on September 1. Although he had remained legally married to his wife, his personal life had become more complex. At the time of his death, he was in the company of a German woman with whom he had developed a close relationship. His daughter, Margret Nissen, later revealed in her 2005 memoir that much of his post-prison life had been dedicated to preserving and promoting the "Speer Myth."

Chapter 5

The Speer myth

After his release from Spandau Prison, Albert Speer carefully crafted and promoted an image of himself as the so-called "good Nazi," a stark contrast to the other high-ranking figures of Hitler's regime who were widely recognized for their brutality. Unlike the stereotypical Nazi war criminals who were seen as fanatical and ruthless, Speer presented himself as an educated, cultured, and rational individual who had been drawn into the Nazi government due to his architectural and administrative skills rather than ideological convictions. This self-fashioned narrative was instrumental in shaping public perception, allowing him to distance himself from the more infamous members of the Nazi hierarchy.

Speer's strategy was incredibly effective. His memoirs and public statements were filled with omissions, distortions, and outright fabrications that painted him as a reluctant participant in Hitler's war machine. His lies became so pervasive and deeply ingrained in public consciousness that historians later described them as the "Speer myths." Even trivial details, such as the circumstances of his own birth, were manipulated to fit his grand narrative. He falsely claimed to have been born at midday to the dramatic sound of crashing thunder and church bells, despite records indicating that his birth occurred in the afternoon and that the church in question had not even been built at the time.

Speer's ability to shape his own myth was amplified by his close collaboration with key figures in the post-war publishing world. Joachim Fest, a prominent historian, and Wolf Jobst Siedler, a leading publisher, played significant roles in the creation and promotion of Speer's memoirs. These men were not merely editors but co-creators of his myth, assisting in the crafting of a narrative that positioned Speer as a noble and apolitical technocrat caught up in events beyond his control. In exchange, they received financial rewards in the form of royalties and other incentives, further cementing their vested interest in maintaining Speer's deceptive image. The result was a masterful piece of historical revisionism that endured for decades despite mounting evidence that exposed the falsity of his claims.

A key component of Speer's self-rehabilitation was his insistence that he had been an "apolitical technocrat" who focused solely on his architectural and administrative duties, unaware of the full extent of the Nazi regime's atrocities. This portrayal was largely accepted by historian Hugh Trevor-Roper, who, in his investigation into Hitler's final days, described Speer as an intelligent but politically disengaged figure. Trevor-Roper characterized Speer as a skilled administrator who was indifferent to politics until the very end of the war when Hitler issued the infamous Nero Decree—an order to destroy Germany's remaining infrastructure. According to Speer, he opposed this order and worked to sabotage its implementation, reinforcing his claim that he had ultimately resisted Hitler's destructive policies.

However, Trevor-Roper also recognized the moral failure in Speer's passive complicity. He noted that, for a decade, Speer had operated at the highest levels of Nazi power, witnessing the regime's crimes firsthand. While he was aware of the inhumane policies being carried out by Hitler's inner circle, he did nothing to intervene. Instead, he focused on his own projects, only taking action when Germany's total destruction threatened his own legacy.

Following Speer's death, historians began to dismantle the myths he had so carefully constructed. Matthias Schmidt's research revealed that Speer had personally ordered the eviction of Jews from their homes in Berlin, directly implicating him in the Nazi regime's policies of persecution. By the late 1990s, numerous historical studies had demonstrated the extent to which Speer had manipulated the truth. However, the public perception of Speer as the "good Nazi" remained relatively intact until 2004, when filmmaker Heinrich Breloer released Speer und Er, a biographical film that critically examined Speer's role in the Nazi government.

This film marked a turning point, initiating a broader reappraisal of Speer's legacy.

Further scholarly investigations, such as those by Adam Tooze and Isabell Trommer, exposed the absurdity of Speer's claims. Tooze argued that Speer was not merely a technocrat passively carrying out orders but a highly ambitious and ruthless political operator who actively maneuvered his way into Hitler's inner circle. Trommer asserted that Speer was not only complicit in Nazi crimes but was, in fact, one of the most powerful and unscrupulous leaders of the regime. Historians such as Martin Kitchen further contended that Speer had successfully deceived both the Nuremberg Tribunal and post-war Germany, portraying himself as an innocent bystander rather than an enabler of Hitler's genocidal policies. Brechtken concluded that if Speer's full involvement in the Holocaust had been revealed at the time of his trial, he likely would have been sentenced to death.

The myth of the "good Nazi" was upheld by several carefully crafted falsehoods. One of the most significant was Speer's repeated insistence that he had been unaware of the Holocaust and the systematic persecution of Jews. This claim was later proven to be completely untrue, as documented evidence showed that he had been present at key meetings where such policies were discussed. Another enduring myth was that Speer had single-handedly revolutionized the German war machine, significantly increasing armaments production and prolonging Germany's ability to fight. While there was some truth to his administrative efficiency, historians later found that his contribution had been exaggerated, as many of the production increases had already been set in motion before his appointment as Minister of Armaments.

Perhaps one of the most audacious lies Speer concocted was a fabricated assassination plot against Hitler. According to this myth, he had supposedly considered using poisonous gas to kill Hitler by directing car fumes into an air ventilation system. This story, which originated from Speer's memory of a brief moment of panic when exhaust fumes accidentally entered a room, was later embellished into a dramatic but entirely fictional assassination attempt.

Speer also falsely claimed to have harbored sympathies for the 20 July 1944 plotters who attempted to assassinate Hitler. He maintained that he had been considered a potential minister in their post-Hitler government, and that Hitler, upon learning of this, became distant toward him. However, historical evidence showed that Speer had remained loyal to Hitler long after the plot failed. Another major distortion was Speer's assertion that he had recognized early on that the war was lost and had worked to preserve resources for Germany's civilian population. In reality, Speer had done everything in his power to extend the war as long as possible, contributing to Germany's massive destruction and loss of life in the final months of the conflict.

Ultimately, Albert Speer's myth-making was one of the most successful historical deceptions of the 20th century. His ability to manipulate public perception allowed him to escape the full consequences of his actions and to be remembered by many as a figure of tragic complexity rather than outright villainy. However, as historical scholarship has shown, Speer was not a misguided technocrat but a key architect of Nazi Germany's war efforts and an enabler of its crimes. His carefully constructed image may have endured for decades, but the truth of his deep complicity in Hitler's regime has since been firmly established.

At the Nuremberg trials and throughout his post-war life, Albert Speer consistently denied having any direct knowledge of the Holocaust. He maintained this position in his memoirs, attempting to absolve himself of personal responsibility while acknowledging only a vague sense of discomfort regarding the Nazi regime's treatment of Jews. In the published version of Spandau: The Secret Diaries, he admitted to feeling uneasy around Jews but stopped short of confessing any knowledge or involvement in their mass extermination. During his final statement at Nuremberg, he carefully framed his words to give the impression of remorse, yet he avoided admitting any direct guilt. Tellingly, the only victims he explicitly mentioned were the German people, ignoring the millions of Jews and other persecuted groups who suffered under the Nazi regime.

Historians have since dismantled Speer's carefully constructed narrative, proving that he was far more than just an innocent technocrat caught up in Hitler's war machine. Martin Kitchen asserts that Speer was "fully aware of what had happened to the Jews" and played a key role in the execution of the so-called "Final Solution." Similarly, historian Magnus Brechtken argues that Speer's occasional, vague admissions of "collective responsibility" were nothing more than a deliberate smokescreen to obscure his direct involvement in Nazi crimes. He strategically accepted limited culpability while steadfastly denying the full extent of his participation.

One of the most damning pieces of evidence against Speer is a photograph taken on March 31, 1943, showing him at Mauthausen concentration camp, surrounded by slave laborers. During this visit, he also toured the nearby Gusen camp. At the Nuremberg trials, Francisco Boix, a Spanish survivor of Mauthausen, testified about Speer's visit, but the incriminating photograph was not available at the time. Historian Telford Taylor later suggested that had this image been presented in court, Speer may have faced the death penalty rather than a prison sentence.

Further evidence emerged in 2005 when The Daily Telegraph reported on newly surfaced documents proving that Speer had personally approved the allocation of materials for expanding Auschwitz. His own assistants had inspected the site on a day when nearly a thousand Jews were murdered. This revelation shattered his long standing claims of ignorance, revealing that he had not only known about the Holocaust but had actively contributed to its infrastructure. Filmmaker Heinrich Breloer, in discussing Speer's role in Auschwitz's expansion, dismissed the idea that he was merely a bureaucratic functionary. Instead, Breloer asserted that Speer was not just a cog in the Nazi machine—he was "the terror itself."

Speer's denials also extended to his presence at the infamous Posen Conference, where Heinrich Himmler openly discussed the extermination of the Jewish people. Speer admitted that he had attended the meeting on October 6, 1943, but claimed to have left the auditorium before Himmler explicitly stated: "The grave decision had to be taken to cause this people to vanish from the earth," followed by the chilling declaration, "The Jews must be exterminated." However, multiple historical records contradict Speer's version of events. Himmler addressed Speer directly during the speech, indicating that he was present for at least some of the most damning statements.

Perhaps the most definitive proof of Speer's knowledge came to light in 2007 when The Guardian uncovered a letter dated December 23, 1971. In this letter, Speer admitted in writing to his longtime correspondent Hélène Jeanty, the widow of a Belgian resistance fighter: "There is no doubt—I was present as Himmler announced on October 6, 1943, that all Jews would be killed." This private admission directly contradicted the public narrative Speer had so carefully maintained for decades.

Despite these overwhelming pieces of evidence, Speer's myth of ignorance persisted for many years. His ability to manipulate public perception, combined with his calculated confessions of limited responsibility, allowed him to escape the full weight of justice. However, as historical research has continued to expose the depth of his complicity, the truth about Speer has become increasingly undeniable. He was not a passive bystander but an active participant in the Nazi regime's crimes, directly enabling the machinery of genocide while meticulously constructing a false image of himself as a remorseful, apolitical architect.

Albert Speer was widely credited with orchestrating an "armaments miracle," a supposed dramatic increase in Germany's war production that kept the country in the fight despite mounting military setbacks. In the winter of 1941–42, following Germany's crushing defeat at the Battle of Moscow, key military and political leaders, including Friedrich Fromm, Georg Thomas, and Fritz Todt, recognized the grim reality: victory was no longer attainable. The logical course of action would have been to negotiate a political settlement to avoid total defeat. However, Speer took a different approach, using his propaganda skills to present an illusion of renewed strength and efficiency within Germany's war economy.

To bolster morale and suppress discussions of surrender, Speer produced exaggerated statistics, claiming a sixfold increase in munitions production and a fourfold increase in artillery output. He ensured these figures reached the public through newsreels, fostering the belief that Germany's military might was still formidable. His messaging successfully curtailed growing concerns about the war's trajectory, at least temporarily.

However, the so-called "armaments miracle" was a carefully constructed myth. While production figures did rise, this was not due to Speer's supposed genius. Instead, it resulted from pre-existing organizational changes, the ruthless exploitation of slave labor, and a shift in manufacturing priorities that sacrificed quality for quantity. By July 1943, the illusion Speer had built was shattered as Germany suffered a series of devastating defeats. The reality of impending loss could no longer be concealed, and his armaments propaganda lost its effectiveness.

Chapter 6

Architectural legacy

Albert Speer's architectural legacy, once envisioned as a grand testament to Nazi power, has largely been erased from modern Germany. Few physical remnants of his designs still exist, leaving behind mostly photographs, blueprints, and scattered ruins. His grand architectural visions, particularly those meant for Hitler's ambitious redesign of Berlin as the world capital, Germania, never came to fruition. Today, only a handful of structures attributed to Speer remain standing, serving as historical artifacts rather than symbols of his architectural prowess.

One of the few surviving remnants of Speer's work in Berlin is the series of four entrance pavilions and underpasses surrounding the Victory Column (Siegessäule). These structures, though relatively minor compared to his grander designs, are among the last traces of his contributions to the city's urban landscape. Another significant, albeit lesser-known, remnant is the Schwerbelastungskörper, a massive concrete cylinder constructed in 1941. This structure, standing 14 meters (46 feet) tall, was not intended as a functional building but rather as an experimental weight-bearing test site. It was used to determine whether Berlin's sandy soil could support the enormous architectural projects Speer had planned, including a colossal triumphal arch that was to dwarf even Paris's Arc de Triomphe. Though the triumphal arch was never built, the Schwerbelastungskörper remains intact, now recognized as a historical landmark and open to the public.

Beyond Berlin, traces of Speer's architectural influence can still be found in Nuremberg, another city central to Nazi propaganda. The Zeppelinfeld stadium, designed by Speer for Nazi rallies, once stood as a grandiose symbol of Hitler's regime. While the stadium's grandstand tribune has been partially demolished, its remains still exist today, standing as a stark reminder of the era. Unlike the fate of many Nazi-era structures, which were deliberately destroyed after the war, portions of the Zeppelinfeld were preserved, both for historical reasons and because demolishing them completely would have been an enormous undertaking.

Speer's most famous project, the New Reich Chancellery in Berlin, was designed to be Hitler's grand seat of power. Completed in 1939, the building was meant to symbolize the dominance and permanence of the Nazi regime, with long marble corridors and opulent meeting halls reflecting Speer's signature aesthetic of intimidating grandeur. However, this symbol of Nazi power did not survive the war. The New Reich Chancellery suffered heavy damage during the Allied bombing campaigns and the brutal fighting of the Battle of Berlin in 1945. While some of its exterior walls remained standing in the immediate aftermath, Soviet forces, upon taking control of Berlin, dismantled the ruins in the post-war years.

There have been persistent but unverified claims that materials from the demolished Reich Chancellery were repurposed for construction projects elsewhere in East Berlin. Some rumors suggest that its red marble was reused in the rebuilding of Humboldt University or in the construction of the Mohrenstraße metro station. Others claim that the Soviets repurposed the remnants for war memorials erected in honor of fallen Red Army soldiers. While no definitive proof has surfaced to confirm these theories, they continue to fuel speculation about how remnants of Speer's grand architectural ambitions may still exist in plain sight, hidden within the fabric of modern Berlin.

Ultimately, Albert Speer's architectural legacy is one of grand aspirations that were never fully realized. His designs, meant to solidify the power and ideology of the Nazi state, have largely been erased or abandoned. The few surviving structures no longer function as monuments to his architectural skill but instead serve as historical sites that remind visitors of a dark chapter in Germany's past. While his blueprints and photographs remain as testament to what could have been, the physical reality of his work has largely been lost to history, leaving behind only fragmented ruins and lingering myths.

Chapter 9

Reflection questions

Speer claimed he was an "apolitical technocrat" who simply followed orders. Do you believe this is a valid excuse, or should individuals always take responsibility for their actions, regardless of their role?

_____

_____

_____

_____

If you were in Speer's position during the Nazi regime, how do you think you would have acted? Would you have resisted, or would you have followed orders out of fear or ambition?

_____

_____

_____

_____

Speer managed to craft a public image of being the "Good Nazi." What does this tell us about how history is shaped by storytelling and personal narratives?

_____

_____

_____

_____

Speer's memoirs allowed him to shift public perception in his favor. How should we approach memoirs or autobiographies when assessing historical truth?

_____

_____

_____

_____

What lessons can be learned from Speer's ability to manipulate public perception? How does this relate to modern politics and media?

_____

_____

_____

Speer was deeply involved in Nazi Germany's war economy, including the use of forced labor. What responsibility do individuals in leadership positions have when they benefit from unethical systems?

Many Germans after World War II claimed they "did not know" the extent of Nazi crimes. Do you think ignorance can be an excuse for inaction, or is it a form of complicity?

Should historical figures be judged by the standards of their time or by universal moral principles? How does this apply to Speer?

Speer admitted to a general sense of guilt but denied personal involvement in the Holocaust. How does selective accountability impact justice and historical truth?

If Speer had been fully transparent about his role in Nazi crimes, do you think history would view him differently today? Why or why not?

Speer was highly intelligent and ambitious, rising quickly in Hitler's inner circle. Can ambition be dangerous if it is not guided by strong moral principles?

What are the dangers of blindly following authority, even when it appears justified at the time?

Speer was able to distance himself from the worst Nazi atrocities by focusing on his work as an architect and minister. What ethical dilemmas exist when professionals separate their expertise from moral considerations?

Are there modern parallels to Speer's role—leaders or professionals who deny responsibility for harmful consequences? What lessons can we take from his story to prevent history from repeating itself?

After his release from prison, Speer made efforts to shape his legacy. Should people be allowed to redefine their past, or does history have an obligation to hold them accountable?

Chapter 10

Lessons learned

Personal Responsibility Cannot Be Ignored : Speer tried to distance himself from Nazi crimes, but history eventually revealed his deeper involvement. This shows that no matter how much one denies responsibility, the truth has a way of emerging.

Ambition Without Ethics Is Dangerous : Speer's rapid rise within the Nazi regime was fueled by his ambition, but he never questioned the morality of his actions. Success without integrity can have devastating consequences.

The Power of Propaganda and Image Control : Speer masterfully crafted the "Good Nazi" myth, showing how powerful narratives can shape public perception, even when they are built on deception.

Denial Does Not Erase Guilt : Despite his claims of ignorance, evidence showed Speer was involved in forced labor and war crimes. Ignoring or downplaying wrongdoing does not absolve someone from accountability.

Moral Blindness Can Lead to Tragedy : Speer focused on his architectural and industrial projects, ignoring the suffering around him. His life demonstrates the dangers of prioritizing personal goals over ethical considerations.

Following Orders Is Not an Excuse : Many Nazis, including Speer, justified their actions by saying they were just following orders.

History has shown that individuals must take responsibility for their choices, even in oppressive regimes.

Historical Truth Will Prevail : For decades, Speer was seen as the "Good Nazi," but deeper investigations exposed his lies. This teaches us that no matter how well-crafted a false narrative is, the truth eventually comes to light.

Complicity in a System of Oppression Has Consequences : Speer was instrumental in Nazi Germany's war machine and used forced labor. Even if he didn't directly participate in mass killings, he enabled the system that committed them.

Redemption Requires Complete Honesty : Speer attempted to portray himself as remorseful, but his selective admissions kept him from true redemption. Genuine atonement requires full transparency and accountability.

The Dangers of Intellectual Arrogance : Speer believed he could outmaneuver other Nazi leaders and later manipulate history. His story highlights the risks of overestimating one's ability to control outcomes.

Evil Thrives When Good People Stay Silent : Speer's silence on Nazi atrocities contributed to immense suffering. His life is a reminder that inaction in the face of evil makes one complicit.

War Crimes Are Never Justified by Efficiency : Speer was praised for his organizational skills, but his "efficiency" came at the cost of human lives. Productivity can never justify moral wrongdoing.

History Judges Actions, Not Intentions : Whether Speer fully believed in Nazi ideology or not, his actions supported the regime. This shows that people are ultimately judged by what they do, not what they claim to believe.

Selective Memory Distorts the Past : Speer's memoirs omitted crucial facts about his role in the Nazi regime. His story teaches us to critically evaluate historical accounts and consider what might be left unsaid.

Legacies Are Built on Truth, Not Lies : Despite Speer's efforts to reshape his legacy, history has largely exposed his deceptions. True legacies endure when they are built on honesty, integrity, and moral responsibility.

Conclusion

As we come to the end of this journey through the life of Albert Speer, I want to take a moment to sincerely thank you. You have invested your valuable time, energy, and resources into reading this book, and that means the world. Without you—the reader—this book would be just words on a page. It is your curiosity, engagement, and willingness to explore history that truly brings this story to life.

Albert Speer's life was one of ambition, deception, survival, and ultimately, reckoning. From his meteoric rise as Hitler's chief architect to his powerful role in the Nazi war machine, and later, his carefully constructed image as the "good Nazi," Speer's story is both fascinating and complex. His time in Spandau Prison, where he walked imaginary journeys around the world and secretly smuggled out his memoirs, shows the resilience of the human mind even in captivity. His post-prison years, spent crafting myths about his innocence, remind us of the power of narrative and how history can be shaped—even manipulated—by those who live it.

The lessons from his life are both cautionary and profound. Speer teaches us about the dangers of blind ambition, the moral compromises that come with power, and the consequences of trying to rewrite history. His role in the Holocaust, which he long denied but was ultimately proven, serves as a reminder that silence in the face of evil is itself a form of complicity. His so-called "armaments miracle," which was more about propaganda than true efficiency, shows us how easily statistics and perception can be manipulated. His architectural legacy, though largely erased, speaks to the grand ambitions of a regime that sought to leave an everlasting imprint on the world—only to be reduced to ruins.

Through it all, Speer's story forces us to ask difficult questions: What would we have done in his position? How much responsibility does an individual bear in a corrupt system? Can someone truly repent for their past, or is accountability more than just words? These are not easy questions, but by reading and reflecting on this book, you have taken a step toward understanding them. And that is powerful.

Your time is valuable, and the fact that you chose to spend it reading this book is something I deeply appreciate. Books like this are not just written—they are read, discussed, and kept alive by people like you. Your engagement gives meaning to these pages, and your thoughts and reflections help keep history relevant for future generations.

If you found value in this book—if it informed you, challenged you, or made you think—I would be incredibly grateful if you could take a moment to leave a positive review. Your feedback not only helps other readers discover this book, but it also supports the work that goes into creating thoughtful, well-researched narratives like this one. A simple review can go a long way in ensuring that these important stories continue to be told.

So, from the bottom of my heart—thank you. Thank you for your time, your curiosity, and your willingness to explore history with an open mind. Your support means everything. I hope this book has left you with new insights, deeper reflections, and a greater understanding of the complexities of history.

Until next time—keep reading, keep questioning, and keep seeking the truth.

Printed in Dunstable, United Kingdom

69115522R00057